The Inheritance Lands

The Inheritance Lands

ANNA KING

RESOURCE *Publications* · Eugene, Oregon

THE INHERITANCE LANDS

Copyright © 2021 Anna King. All rights reserved. Except for brief quotations in critical publications or reviews, no part of this book may be reproduced in any manner without prior written permission from the publisher. Write: Permissions, Wipf and Stock Publishers, 199 W. 8th Ave., Suite 3, Eugene, OR 97401.

Resource Publications
An Imprint of Wipf and Stock Publishers
199 W. 8th Ave., Suite 3
Eugene, OR 97401

www.wipfandstock.com

PAPERBACK ISBN: 978-1-6667-3348-8
HARDCOVER ISBN: 978-1-6667-2814-9
EBOOK ISBN: 978-1-6667-2815-6

NOVEMBER 15, 2021 8:37 AM

For Mom, Aralyn, and Cade

Contents

Acknowledgements | ix

Part I.

anorexia | 3

cleaning | 6

cannot | 8

wedding | 11

source | 14

finale | 17

edge | 19

Part II.

unseen | 23

failings | 25

immovable | 27

discharge | 28

agreement | 31

new | 33

Part III.

May | 39

example | 41

Evelyn Amelia | 43

Ponce Inlet Lighthouse | 45

single | 47

tenant | 50

here | 52

repayment | 54

domain | 57

Acknowledgements

Thank you to my beloved Abba, whose faithfulness outlasts all fear and sickness. These lands are good because you gave them to me. Help me continue to steward them well.

Mom, you have modeled walking alongside wounded children bent on self-destruction. I am grateful for your wisdom, your place in my home, and market runs.

My darling Aralyn Kaytie—I am humbled to share in this narrative with you. Your thoughts and insights are chiseled into every poem, and I treasure your trust to publish this. The pain is only part of the arc, my love.

Cade Gregory, what would I do without you to make me laugh and to ensure we see all the little things together? You are my lion and my lamb.

Pastor Caleb Land was my first reader of the work on behalf of my church. I am proud to be part of a congregation that fans the fires of creativity and art in service of Jesus.

My church, Southpoint, did a beautiful series in the summer of 2021 on the Psalms. Thank you Pastor Mark Howell, Pastor Chris Brown, Pastor Caleb Land, Pastor

Acknowledgements

Michael Powell, and Pastor Geoff Cauble. Those sermons led way to the book title, as well as the section names.

The Fine Arts Department at Eagle's Landing Christian Academy, directed by Chuck Ekstedt, deserves my heartfelt thanks for sponsoring the first round of publishing costs. I am honored to teach at a school that values art.

Part I.

*"Hear my cry, O God; listen to my prayer.
From the ends of the earth I call to you"*

PSALM 61:1

anorexia

To get to the Walden clinic,
we slice through Atlanta traffic
thick, clogged
an hour each way.
The sunsets siphon
our breath at night after the clock
moves forward an hour—
a sky can be the color of coral and amber.

Three meals a day. Three
snacks. Three hours between. Three
food groups at each meal (protein starch produce). Three
caloric beverages. Three
people left in the house:
a mother and two children.

We keep her story small, she and I—
I show her how to share facts:
*Medical reasons. This. That is what
I need. We will communicate as it shifts.*
She gives the nurse her lunch I pack,
thinks of ideas I do not,
asks me to insist she make her bed
so she can see order when she comes
home at night.

One teacher presses, and my daughter cannot
eat dinner. I want warfare—
rage in my mouth like cement.

She lets me call a meeting
then finds her voice:
*She just kept on and then
I blurted out why I have to leave each week!*
The principal's eyes go wide.

Conniving with the addiction,
she'll contort at times,
the disorder imploding
her with shame and she clamps
lips, defiant of losses accompanying refusal.
I take her out of ballet,
will cut her off after an hour, plate it
for the next time.

Some days she finishes,
time to spare, chirping and
worryless.

Thirteen, her mind unfurls spiders
furrowing, vicious.
*You may be angry all you want.
If you do not eat,*

*your life will stop. I'm not
in a hurry.*
She's sat in the curves of my bent
legs, asleep from the strain
of pushing back. I hold her hand sometimes
when she fights herself
to eat the rest
of the cheesecake, porkchops with mango salsa.
*Sweetheart, you are still here
after you got it down.*

The girl across the table at treatment
hovered over a cookie.
Aralyn hugged her when she
won,
the crumbs remaining brown, soft.

cleaning

Chad doesn't want the garden—doesn't know if he'll return.
Will help with advice. Will allow
me to use whatever I need of his still in our home.

Sundays, the table is black and long.
We three position where we always eat, the fourth
chair vacant.

He left the night before we buried
Memaw, a Friday in January.
My vision funneled, muscles bogs.

A week before he goes, Aralyn whispers
with fence-like teeth she cannot
eat. Our strain I thought invisible helped gag her.

When he was here, I learned to explain when I re-arranged,
to clarify nothing was gone,
that it helped me if food storage made

more sense. I would not touch
what was solely his, leaving
his domain, often dusty, crowded.

Then the air warmed, buttery and floral,
weeds choking the asparagus bed,
compost unturned, hydrangeas

woody, unpruned. His worm farm
dies, starved. I didn't know
how to feed them, too tired

to learn. When Cade is gone on Saturdays,
I start to clean the garage, the junk drawers,
bought new batteries for flashlights

rusty and disused. The shelves, they
clear for garden baskets, for crates
of eggs I've saved. I throw away nothing

of his, just move it, discover
lost screwdrivers, seed packets,
first aid supplies, hummingbird feed.

My brother Jonathan showed me how
to use the blower when he cleaned the gutters,
but I've forgotten, so I sweep

the piles and piles, like brown anthills,
until no more dirt can track
into the house.

cannot

He agreed to build the
chicken run, coop completed last weekend,
told me I can have the four
Rhode Island Reds,
already paid for, ready
for pickup.

He will work from our house since
I am away at school
when a window needs repair, leaving
a receipt for the job he paid for.
Do you need me to help with that?
I ask and he says no.

Cade has new clothes and shoes,
talks of a Spiderman room
in an apartment his Dad will get
that I know nothing of.

He does the yard each week,
faithfully
pays the mortgage.
He'll get the mail,
take out trash, wash clothes,
put away dishes
in the later hours I'm away

at treatment with Aralyn.
She watches concrete
when he leaves, his wave
not meant for her.

Thought this would make you smile
I say of the picture from the wedding
he did not attend with me. The text
descends into a gulf of quiet.

Are you willing to explain
why you are not wearing your ring?
He is not.

Some days, he will not look
me in the eye, desperate and choking
to exit, duty done
to pick up on time.
He'll linger unexpectedly, tell of
his Mom's heart condition,
the nausea of disciplining Cade.

Look, we both have a lot
going on in our lives. I want you
to know underneath it all, I still
love you.
He is a wordless mountain, a well leading to the ocean.

My prayers shift away from the plans,
from the promises. They are chants
for a dead man, spawned of grief
unfurling into the last stage:
acceptance.

*Give me courage to let go,
for nothing else but trust.
I do not see Your good.*

wedding

My youngest brother marries
in March, his bride
Christina gorgeous. Tender
hearted, she arrived to care
for my children on days I am unable
to arrange help.

Maria, Christina's mother, gave me *Jesus Calling*
at her bridal shower weeks before. I'd quietly
searched for Aralyn when she disappeared
into the bathroom. Vacant, she refused
to touch a cupcake.
Maria's youngest, clawed by depression,
had ribs emerge like branches.
Maybe this book can help you, too.
And it will all be ok.
I cried in her hallway—
lilac crescents under my eyes.

My navy dress, a single shoulder
like my wedding,
needs no alternation that spring.
Months without wine
flattened me,
already crafted
from the weights and pull ups—

the warfare against the vortex.
Not even at their wedding? Mom presses.
I resist the deafness the ferment
brings to the empty
place at tables, at funerals, at counseling appointments.
Not even tonight, I say.

They stand under the trellis,
white scarves on the arbor
whirling in a breeze.
The pastor reminds marriage came before
other covenants.
My chest becomes marble.
Nothing has been signed
with us.

My son Cade, three, a ring-bearer
stands between his uncles.
He waves over and over, thrilled to see me
watch him doing well.
Jonathan, the middle, assured he would
watch my son so I can make it through
that night.
This might be depression,
I told him. I had dragged myself
from bed to come,
nearly suffocating
at Chad's fewer clothes in the closet
since Friday afternoon.

Aralyn will not eat the wedding dinner, jaw
granite when she lost sight of us,
thinking we were
swallowed by the river behind the venue.

The scarlet dress will not
hide her arms, her legs,
wraithlike marble people admire,
yet her terror in the mirror.
We shout in the car ride home, ragged,
You are the only person I have!
And how do you think it feels to have everything on me?
You don't listen to how feel!
You can't take away that I get frustrated when its hard!
You don't know what it's like to have an eating disorder!
You can't expect me to fix it!
You don't know that I'm scared because they never come back!
We know the ashes of charting abandonment.

Black mascara veins her cheeks.
My love, we have what we need for today.
We will keep going,
and look at who is still here.
God withholds nothing from us,
even when people do.

She eats a dinner, fastfood and awful,
and sleeps.

source

She's been allowed to act this way!
Chad would insist, eyes obsidian,
glittering hard, militant.

If you gave her attention, she'd stop
he'd say, my anger wrapped
around my throat, overwhelmed. I work
a job, choking in the marriage,
trying to finish graduate school.
Sometimes he's on her side.

You have another child, you know
he reminded, teeth
clenched after I'm away with her.
No time eases
her fear, that millstone. She grabs
at me, sinking, day after day.

After we are married, she is not
sleeping in bed with us, he tells me.
I drag her, defiant and unusual, far too old,
back to her bed night
after night before we marry.
She learns to lie
awake, quiet, sleepless,
in her own room.

If he's away, she sleeps
with me. I bite back

guilt at her slow morning starts.
I don't know if what I demand
is within her realm.
She asks to drink coffee at twelve,
and I let her in case it helps.

What now?
he'd grumble, another injury, another
sickness the beginning
scenes of her month-long panics.
She and I go to
the ER once, she too knotted
to drink, dehydrated
from the flu.
She'll wear the brace, the cast,
take the pills exactly
as the experts say. I learn
to let others do the talking:
No, Dr. Hodges says this will hurt, but
you must do it to get better.

I have her write her terrors,
share them with her counselor. I buy
her essential oils, massages,
sleep aids, bring her to exercise,

chart her sleep with an Ipad.
I take her phone at night,
keep a routine, cook healthy,
give her vitamins.

She tries. She tries. She tries.

*You gave me this child. Let me accept
her as you made her. You saw
fit to take
these men away. Show me
how to stay inside the gaps.*

Four months since he left, we see
a psychiatrist.
Crippling anxiety, she calls it,
and OCD. She's frozen
into patterns, wilting of ceaseless terror.
Later, ADHD as well.
Aralyn cannot use the therapy,
the eating disorder treatment,
without medication. Dr. G. doesn't often have this
as her first step.

As we filled out the charts, I
joke we win
all the marks in family history.

*You have tried
everything. This is not your fault,*
Dr. G tells me in private.
Stones inside
my lungs drop—thudding
with the tears I loosen
for the prison she has lived inside.

finale

At times he comes back to me a little, timid, funny,
sends a picture
of Cade's outfit choice
while I grocery shop.

It won't last, I tell my friend. *I don't know
how to love him in absence.* I twist
when I have him, a schism between
relief, hurt.
I want him here
all the time. I throb
with a child disintegrating.

He must show me the chicken run,
though it's dark and rainy,
peppering me a to-do list:
dust bath, herbs they eat, one day a larger
coop. He jokes Cade tried to help,
that's why the roof is lopsided.
He uses the word *we*.

I thank him.
I show him our new cat,
his heart soupy
with animals. His hand was shredded
when he saved his dog
from an attack. He cleaned her wounds
for months,
relentless in his care.

I'd held his hand when we put her down,
cancer throbbing
in her skull. He would not
get another.

He kneels to see the kitten, a nest
under the bicycle.
Cosette is fuzzy, brown and fragile,
his face eases.
He filled the doorway,
satisfied he was useful,
tired at the late hour we come back
from the clinic.

It's stage 3, he says. We *will know soon
if it's stage 4.*

He says he does not want
to acknowledge our anniversary.

edge

I've never lived inside this pit,
I write to myself in my journal.

Color drains from the world
sometimes.
The terror
of this domain He gives
stretches through nights, my mind
punctured by insomnia.

Anorexia murders the most
of mental illness,
intersects all
ethnicity, males and females
intertwines with anxiety,
trauma.

Angry, I seethe to Him
Why am I always the only one left?
The rage behind
my teeth is clay.

You are not,
He says. My palms unfold.
The lies can fit so snugly,
like a noose.

We've stayed on
repeat, shattered things of
wounds glistening and seeping,
cycles of the past.

*I want Daddy to know when
he left, it hurt me!* Aralyn shouted
after family therapy at the clinic.
And Chad did too!

Tears cluster
in my eyes and I set
my palm against a scarecrow
shoulder of my child.
Me too.

Was there ever
another way?

*Darling, have
your pain. Then take your hands
off their throats. Ask God to help
pry your fingers off.
What comes next
can be your choice.*

So it is to accept

all of this—and release it
to be recast.

Part II.

*"But I trust in your unfailing love;
my heart rejoices in your salvation"*

PSALM 13:5

unseen

Are you done?
I ask. He won't attend counseling when I request.
Venomous, he shouts,
Did you think I would come back?

Accepting love is a choice
the therapist had said.
Please, please can we just try?
my tears uncurling.
My white knuckled politeness
crumbles, egg shells beneath a hammer.
*We made a promise, Chad. We made
a promise.*

He'd rather be living with his parents,
40, see his son when he can.

Five months after
Chad leaves, I whorl on the bedroom
rug, alone. He'd emptied drawers
weeks ago, left shaving cream and the hair dryer.

Mom suggested I pray for him as
myself. So I ask to see beyond
an anger veil, words harsh, the ebbing
of seven years of turmoil.

Cade holds my hand, fingers curled
through mine at the pharmacy.
Major Depression. Recurrent.
General Anxiety Disorder.
My doctor wrote.
The pills are small, halved
for now, coral.
The doctor said to hold off
on marital decisions until
it's been long enough,
I explained. He presses his lips, half
nods.

failings

Aralyn and her father and I, we drag
fingers down the list
at the clinic,
on those paragraphs of inner demons
driving people to destruct.

Aralyn mutters *acceptance*.
Gnawed alive,
she self-flagellates, threading
her own flesh, always colored by garnet ribbons.
*She's a spearwoman if
someone else hurts*, I tell the counselor,
my palm gentle on her wrist.
After our dog died,
she sold dozens of cookies from our freezer,
donated $150 to the shelter.

Jonny, quiet, cavern deep,
clears his throat and says,
Forgiveness. Laser eye on
mistakes, errors—
especially his own.
My muscles knot,
at my judgment
of alcoholism, of the missing child support,
of the moves to new places hundreds
of miles away.
Empathy, I claim. *Gently accepting of feelings,
to consider another side.*

Oh my anger at her disintegration,
missing my son, her acting
out so much worse with me,
6 meals a day—late nights from the hour drive
and her failure to choose getting better.

immovable

My heels spike into dirt
to the disease that wants my girl.
I'll give you your choices
but not your death.
I slow her world,
require yoga, more chores,
time at home, gentle reassurances to worry,
consequences to not asking
for help.
Her father and I do things like take her door
off the hinges
when she cannot be trusted.
We make amends
for a decade.
The weeks crosshatch
with visits to the clinic,
long after when most people leave.
I know all their names. One family
gives us a hamster.

She relapses in fall. I take her to residential next,
pull her out of school and the musical—
keep her there through Christmas, New Year,
Valentine's Day
shrink her world to the choice to eat or not,
hold her hand when a soft-spoken nurse presses a tube
through her nose.

discharge

Thoughts always change last,
Lautesha, the case manager, once assured.
Some just need us to give them more time.

The medication, woven into neurons now,
curls around my thoughts,
gentling, stilling them.
I can set aside tasks I do not
need, terror and turmoil at the undone
loosened.
My son brings me a leaf, yellowed and stiff,
and I must put it on display.
I am present, a laughing mother, no longer
plagued with 1,000 projects
or unsolved problems.
I love my children like I did
my five brothers and sisters growing up—
those layers of my hearts.

I've learned calm to the disease,
a fortress to it—a stone to its demands,
control, lying. Our home does not
wheel around sickness now.

It is then my daughter
asks to cook dinner. Stops resisting
plating her food. Bathes her brother for me.
Watches for the next
snack time. Connects

to a show I like and insists I start it
from the beginning with her so
she can share it with me.
She leads in group therapy sessions.

I cull each word, each thought, each choice—
Abba, does this bring peace?

My daughter, so gentle and broken,
can see the inner chasms of hurt
especially when I do not say it.
I assure her of divorce talk
I choose you. I always will. I will not leave.
We can drive
without words,
if I say before,
Honey, today I am grieving.

She lets me put my hand around
hers when her report card
of the year dips from a lifetime of
perfection.
*The best of you is
not on this paper, my love.*

Nor was it in the photos
I took down
of a wedding.

*Mom, I think I am a pomegranate
with faith,* she says. *Don't those take forever
to be ready?*

*They do need longer, but
it's just the right amount,* I tell her.
We have to wait for them.

agreement

I would like to have a conversation
about next steps
he says on Thursday.

The cycle begins sewing
into my chest, pinpricking darts
hot and constant.
I text my friend Ezel,
I'm afraid whenever he asks
to talk.
You must learn to hear him,
she says, or *there is no chance at all.*
What can you do to hear?

Ask questions to make sure
you understand, my therapist says.
Repeat back. Verify.
Hear Chad, not your fear.

I let Aralyn's Dad stay
for the second half of treatment Thursday, ask he bring
her home so I can leave,
mounting pressure to hear Chad.
I'm tired from a cold,
coughing, ragged, ready to up the sleeping dose
to the max the doctor advised.

She tells me later her Dad wept to her on the way home
his regret he ever left,
was an alcoholic, suicidal, but always tried to choose her.

The blue couch fabric presses against
a shirt he's bought
since he's left.

Gentled, bloomed,
I'd prayed for hours, listened
to music, limited
tasks. I grapple hard, choose being present.

We try this summer, maybe,
to go back to counseling.
I will get an apartment anyways.
He knows his cannot
do well at his parents,
the tug of destructive behavior he shuns.

I nod, willing to let it unfurl.

new

As a girl, I
marveled at people with eyes
that did not blink and whose breathing did not
change with tension.

Before, my throat eroded, brain thrashing, blood
embedded. I'd misplace
a PhD, memorize a floor and all its patterns.
I'd fix. I'd fix. I'd fix.
I forgot my gathered facts, couldn't summon
alternatives or ask
for contribution.

Nauseated or reeling or sleepless—
I tangled like slashed lace
whenever there was anger.

A hot afternoon he
said he would not attend
the marriage retreat—my last
olive branch, his answer
a seven-year *no*.
I set the phone down, stones around my clavicle.
My friend Becky nodded, her mouth a line.
The kids finished lunch, swam
some more in her pool
outside her blue house.
And I did not die.

That fall, I would sign divorce papers
I filed—and paid the entire fee.
I left the small brick office and went
back to work, because
it carried on.
The students ask, *Where were you!*
I shrug, *A meeting.*
But we are going to finish Beowulf.
Take out those books!

Piles of boxes made Tetris
in the garage and I told him he had two weeks.
He snarled at arrival,
refused my help to load and I
smiled and went inside.

I threw away old fishing poles and bikes
that cluttered months
after the house remained mine. My skin stayed cool
when he insisted they were from his childhood. It had been
18 months since
he left.

I went on
to buy new rugs
to replace the creaking storm door
to rip up shoddy laminate
to undo and then repair garden walls
to stop littering counters
to get rid of abstract metalwork over the fireplace
to organize inside the shed
to not have 12 screwdrivers
to have someone else care for the yard so I could rest
to have friends for dinner

to sleep without meds
to renovate two bathrooms
to complete financials goals (all except a paid off house)
to grow an orchard
to write a novel
to raise chickens
to nearly empty the attic
to join a church
to take naps on Saturday.

The story now holds more than
loss.

When a quiz at church says I'm born to lead,
I chuckle.
Yes, I'm pouring forth—

into these vineyards, these lands,
once wilderness, once Egypt.

My body is not a nest
of knots, peace threaded through
me, a tapestry through seasons when
He was always good.

I tasted the air of my own space
like nectar,
breathing not changing now.

Part III.

*"You have guarded all that is mine.
The land you have given me is a pleasant land.
What a wonderful inheritance!"*

PSALMS 16:5−6

May

This time in Georgia, we didn't skip
ahead to summer. Spring drifted in—
distracting, luscious, beckoning.

Hard green knots weigh down
the peach tree limbs. I didn't know
the marigold seeds I sprinkled

like confetti would rupture
over an entire raised bed.
Mom worries we need to transplant

the unexpected guests and I ask
for more time: *Let's just wait
until we know for sure what they look like.*

I eat the first blueberry, pulling away
the netting that keep the birds off, threatening
the dog if he sneaks under the fence again.

The sweet peas take their time, their little
white Pilgrim caps mingling
with the sneaky ripened pods

my son and I eat right away, ignoring
the roughened, uneven cypress mulch
of a golden-brown flooring under our feet.

As days warm, I let God
unclench my fists around wisps
of men who did not stay.

example

So here's the outer scene:
one wall is fuchsia—I didn't pick the color—the carpet
gray, the stains not from *anyone* in my class,
of course. Counters line the walls,
posters hovering over that say *Smart People Read*
and *Everyone Learns Differently*. The oldest is
Be the Change You Want to See in the World—I bought
it before my first day thirteen years ago, the same
words in the rooms of my children at home.
The clock will glitch and my fan is tilted.

By 7th period, they are wired, desperate,
on edge for 3:15. Friday, I'm the gatekeeper
of the weekend. Dillon and Colton learn how
to pierce ceiling tiles
with paper footballs. *You are not leaving until
you get those down!*
Jesus, help me the day before holidays.

They are eclectic, sweet, sincere, connected.
Eirini learns
a new language with us, diligent in every
task, her artwork beautiful, cross-cultural thoughts
stunning.
Bryce soaks
ideas in quickly, processing

and applying. He's the first
to write a sonnet and never

struggles to meet the page length. He giggles
time and again when my son complains about school.
Colton, socks always showing, is never scared
of testing out my questions, undaunted. His prayer
requests center around family.
Dillon's tight black curls
burst from his head like coils. He
puts the room at ease, brilliant
at catching onto the themes.
Jada, hair like a magazine cover, with a nose stud
that isn't clear, greets me daily
and never has a cruel word about anyone.
Ethan, who grew a foot in months, leaves early
for cross country, where he dazzles. 10th grade year
he sinks his teeth into his grades,
wanting an A so badly he salivates.
Bri sends me Google hangout messages even
during Covid, peppered with ideas for projects. She convinces me
about Crocs and I buy a pair. She loves when
romance infiltrates our literature.

They are in year two
of four with me, should
they stay. We become
 a little woven group—not minding at times
if class is over, keep talking.
With them, the days slip
by quickly, raindrops on a pane.

They'll write this summer on messages
in images, examining our digital culture,
and I'll
be awaiting their return.

Evelyn Amelia

When I first saw my own children
at their births,
snail tongues, mewling like goats,
I did not know tears and breath
could tear out from a body's deepest places
like that.

They told us in June they were
expecting, my brother and his wife—
who've agreed to take my children if something
ever happened to me.
I erupt, dazed, light, laughing
at the news
to love another's baby.

She twists up in the womb like spaghetti,
situating breached, hips displaced,
the cord wrapping
around her neck. They expedite her
entrance with a knife,
No one comes
February 16th
since it's the pandemic.

We drive
the hour to bring them dinner at home, Mom and I,
bags loaded, lists checked off, fretting
too much about if we got enough.

Jonathan stands between gray walls,
arm crooked with her, a smile into
his eyes as well.

She's miniscule, face squished,
eyes blue like mountains.
I did not know tears and breath
could tear out from a body's deepest places
like that
again.

Ponce Inlet Lighthouse

He won't let me read many signs, tugs my hand and wants
his picture in front of the terracotta
cone before we go inside.
Those black stairs whorl
ceilingward and my son
looks at me with cavern eyes. He insists
he is not scared of Florida's
Tallest Lighthouse. The metal rail
is clammy and I feel fright
on our behalves. He can do it himself
as he glides up and I hover
a step behind in case
he stumbles. The floor is a checkerboard
beneath.

Five years old, absorbing an afternoon
with only me, he scrambles and darts
like a rabbit
in the blustery morning after I pay
the admission fee to the museum and
village.
He's a cheap date to the cracker cottages
and huge rusted anchors.

We peer at old lighthouse lenses saved,
all taller than he,

cut into panels and perched behind the ropes,
purpose ancient and useful.

At the top, the wind is gnawing. I film the view
for family and he adds
to my narration *It's like we can see the whole world!*
His flag on his red Old Navy shirt
ripples and I insist we make it short up there.
We eat lunch in the car. He chatters and he
chatters. He'll let me press my palm to his cheek
and hugs me in reply—
Did you enjoy the day, Love?

single

Reasonable, healing, patient, aloof
as a pyramid (like Becky advises), I activate
an online dating profile.

I filter for Christian men close by, taller than me,
who exercise and smile in photos.
I'm fine with children,
not "discreet relationships."

I vet the complainers, the cursing,
the demanders, the passives, the bullies,
the beer in every photo-ers, the conversation
fizzlers, the ones who say
ur hot wanna meet?

One guy doesn't list his religion, snarls
when I ask of it.
Kinda judgey, aren't you?
I say I did not mean to offend, wish him
a good day.

Another insists on his faith
but then confesses spiritual "trances."
I cancel that phone call
when Ezell says *No one does that! It's weird!*

Half-Dominican Justen ghosts after three dates. I don't bother
asking why. He made it to Facetime
with Aralyn.
He buys me some nice art prints
I put up in the bathroom anyways.

Brandon with the tattoo sleeve insists
we meet until I relent, says his schedule is clear
for next week too, and doesn't
follow up.

Jed texts madly
when I'm on vacation and I
call it off—*we are searching
for different levels of closeness.*

Army Aaron sets the time and place,
wants to change it all an hour before.
In the car with make up fresh, kids dropped off,
GPS activated, I decline.
*Thanks for your service to the military.
Wish you the best.*

Tom and I made plans,
but
he's jealous my favorite
Marvel hero is Thor,
peppers later texts
with acid. I do not go after all.
You really need to do nothing,
Judith Lockhart says, eyebrows
bossy. *God will send him
and it won't be because of you.*

But control is my favorite!
I insist.

Six months later, app reactivated, I agree to
meet Dave after graduation.
He drives to me,
holds the door, is polite
to the waiter—
talks about himself the entire time
then gives me a business card.
I text a *thank you for dinner* later,
that *I did not feel a connection*.

I delete the profile after one week back.

I've decided to love Jesus and Cade,
I tell Emily.

tenant

The first time—
a joke.
I widened
my eyes, sitting on fireplace bricks
pressing into my hamstrings.
She, on my blue couch, watches
me, data gathering.
All I have is the sunroom anyways!

The second time—
my youngest sister Adria, hair dark
like mine, fierce
and layered with ambition too,
sat on the blue couch as well. Mom
swirled her wine, words
tight, even
though she knew who to ask.
*Well I sure don't have room
in my apartment!* Adria observes.
She knew
this was coming, delighted
to watch the scene.
But all I have is the sunroom, you know,
I splutter, the notion a hurricane of change.
Adria unravels
in laughter.

Well just for a few months!
Mom offers—promising
to help with cooking.
Oh I know she means
forever. It took years
to sell the house
once all six kids were gone,
widowed and losing money on it.
She settles in the familiar
like a nest.

I let it be our joy to have her,
to be given enough
to give what I can.

My sister has not
stopped laughing, follows close behind.
Hooray! Let's go
look at my
new room!
Now you are going to have to
get rid
of some of this stuff.

Mom starts to buy me wine
and I agree to have some.

here

She's coming for you, Anna!
Adria texts
the night before the move.

Mom sends me articles on
the benefits of grandparents,
insists she will do the groceries.

I fix
the sagged door,
install a hook for her robe,
come help her find a place for everything.
I learn to close the door
to her room,
the space whirlwind like the home
I knew before I left at twenty.
I give Mom timelines on completing
tasks, write out checklists
she leaves on counters
and I text a picture of.
I simplify the tidy—
leave her items that confetti
the house on the dining room table
so she'll put them away:
coffee cups dog leashes sunglasses laundry baskets vitamins paperwork shoes jackets boxes phone chargers earrings hats baby clothes for Evelyn books hair brushes make up umbrellas.

Once she found a flute in her room.
She gives to Aralyn,
gleeful and smug to grant a wish.
Aren't you glad I save things, Anna Rebekah?
We marvel, mouths
stunned like fish—*where did you get this?*
I save things! she sings, pushing aside
the box of ammo
with her toe.

Months unwind. She's going nowhere.
Loves her friends nearby,
visiting the Square,
doing the garden with me.
Cade snuggles to listen to her
Bible stories about David or
see old photos of uncles who look
like him.

She brings the family dog
Cade adores,
Drake's white hair dotting his clothes.
I intervene
when she does all of Aralyn's laundry—
Mom, she has to learn to do everyday life!
She still sneaks
washing Aralyn's sheets.

This is so ridiculous I tell my girl,
who shows all her teeth in that delighted grin.

repayment

The character of a Christian
is hospitality
Pastor Caleb challenges,
and love costs
time and energy and money.

I've been uncurling, petals
wide and sunlight drinking—
my granite within
ebbed away like oil spreading fingers out.

How does our home give back?
I ask them, fork dangling
in my right hand. Their brows furrow.
The kids and I agree:
keep our home tidy, share dinner,
give food away, pray when we know of pain,
listen, speak of gratitude, use words of kindness,
see people
beneath the ugliness of wounds
we know are not the end of the story.
People will not see Him
if we do not show them.

And, they do come.
Some bid, others not.
No one tenses anymore
with knocks.
Our white plates

all get used. I don't
put away the extra chairs.

Or we go.

We help people move,
feed the fish, drop off dinner,
clean houses for tired mothers,
catch loose dogs, bring clothes
for the newly fostered.

It is well
over our doorway is our anthem.
Because we are,
we see who is not.

Women find me, secret with their pain—
with eating disorders
gnaw daughters,
or terrified and pregnant,
with husbands who cannot see them,
fearful of counseling
that will mine those old terrors,
of a child who cannot
be put back together.
My heart is water for them.
You must learn tools—
even alone if needed.
He will make
this into good, but
you must
let Him.

I unhand the ashes, show them
beauty followed,
that I could have learned no other way

domain

— for Nathan

This season, it is no longer waiting—
for the next argument, the next
starvation, the next
leaving, the next anger, the next
sleepless month, the next chaos.

Aralyn cooks now, swirling
gnocchi bubbling in creamy
hills, unsure of how to season chicken
but plates it for all of us.
Every Friday we eat nachos.
She and I savor the breadth
of epic poetry, name
our new kitten Circe.

Cade and I
challenge each other's *always* and *never*. He likes
to hold my hand when we go for walks,
insists we go together to check
on the slender pencils
of green beans.
We read Narnia,
he tugging my elbow crook
for the next page.

I tell Mom I will build her
a garage apartment, a gift
of permanency. Her eyes go

wide at this.

A good man asks me out, one who
loves Jesus—what I know now
cannot be another way.
His blue eyes are clear
of rage. He is a teacher,
kind to his mother and sister.

In the curve of my hammock,
faded purple and yellow, I
watch a sky from my own yard,
the notion pressed into my ribs.

You have given me much, I pray.
The enormity of this
kingdom spans out,
rich and intricate,
thriving like grasses
on a field.
I sway in summer air—
Is this next?

The olive tree
this year knots finally with fruit,
the pomegranates
cluster in waxy scarlet.

He has given me
peace, gracious and good
to us. We thrive
now, tended, slowed, gentle
to each other.

July simmers evening
air when Chad finally touches the ache
of what he left behind—eyes
dark now with weeping.
I release him
as our remedy,
of my own palms
around his throat.
We are well now. You can be too.

I once tore at the world
with teeth,
relentless to improvement,
coaxing challenge out of
stones. Now I add nothing,
ruthless for the goodness I already
have been given.

Guard them, the Lord says.
You are not alone.
I never have been.

www.ingramcontent.com/pod-product-compliance
Lightning Source LLC
Chambersburg PA
CBHW061510040426
42450CB00008B/1550